BOOK JOURNAL

BOOK
JOURNAL

HARPER PERENNIAL
London, New York, Toronto and Sydney

Harper Perennial
An imprint of HarperCollins*Publishers*
77–85 Fulham Palace Road
Hammersmith
London W6 8JB

www.harperperennial.co.uk

This edition published by Harper Perennial 2006

9 8 7 6 5 4 3 2 1

Copyright © HarperCollins 2006

A catalogue record for this book is
available from the British Library

ISBN-13 978-0-00-724028-9
ISBN-10 0-00-724028-7

Set in PostScript Linotype Minion with Spectrum Display by
Rowland Phototypesetting Ltd, Bury St Edmunds, Suffolk

Printed and bound in Great Britain by Butler & Tanner Ltd, Frome

LITERARY PRIZES

THE MAN BOOKER PRIZE

This UK-based literary prize rewards the writer of the best novel of
the year written by a citizen of the Commonwealth or the Republic of
Ireland. The Man Booker judges are selected from the country's best
critics, writers and academics, and the prize is awarded every October at
a star-studded event.
www.themanbookerprize.com

WINNERS

2005   *The Sea* · John Banville

2004   *The Line of Beauty* · Alan Hollinghurst

2003   *Vernon God Little* · D B C Pierre

✓ 2002   *Life of Pi* · Yann Martel

2001   *True History of the Kelly Gang* · Peter Carey

入 2000   *The Blind Assassin* · Margaret Atwood

1999   *Disgrace* · J M Coetzee

1998   *Amsterdam* · Ian McEwan

1997   *The God of Small Things* · Arundhati Roy

1996   *Last Orders* · Graham Swift

1995   *The Ghost Road* · Pat Barker

1994   *How Late It Was, How Late* · James Kelman

1993   *Paddy Clarke Ha Ha Ha* · Roddy Doyle

ORANGE PRIZE FOR FICTION

Set up in response to the concern that the prize's founders felt that women's writing was often overlooked, the woman-only, UK-based Orange Prize has been going since 1996. The winner is announced in June. www.orangeprize.co.uk

WINNERS

2006	*On Beauty* · Zadie Smith
2005	*We Need to Talk About Kevin* · Lionel Shriver
✓ 2004	*Small Island* · Andrea Levy
✓ 2003	*Property* · Valerie Martin
✓ 2002	*Bel Canto* · Ann Patchett
✓ 2001	*The Idea of Perfection* · Kate Grenville
2000	*When I Lived in Modern Times* · Linda Grant
1999	*A Crime in the Neighbourhood* · Suzanne Berne
1998	*Larry's Party* · Carol Shields
✓ 1997	*Fugitive Pieces* · Anne Michaels
1996	*A Spell of Winter* · Helen Dunmore

COSTA BOOK AWARDS
(formerly the WHITBREAD PRIZE)

This prize is open to British authors and has five categories, from which the final winner is chosen by a panel of nine judges.
www.costabookawards.com

WINNERS

2005	*Matisse: The Master* · Hilary Spurling	
2004	*Small Island* · Andrea Levy	
2003	*The Curious Incident of the Dog in the Night-Time* · Mark Haddon	
2002	*Samuel Pepys: The Unequalled Self* · Claire Tomalin	
2001	*The Amber Spyglass* · Philip Pullman	
2000	*English Passengers* · Matthew Kneale	
1999	*Beowulf* · Seamus Heaney	
1998	*Birthday Letters* · Ted Hughes	
1997	*Tales from Ovid* · Ted Hughes	
1996	*The Spirit Level* · Seamus Heaney	
1995	*Behind the Scenes at the Museum* · Kate Atkinson	

PULITZER

The longest running of all literary prizes has been going since 1917. Its 21 categories are open to US citizens or those writers published in a US newspaper for the journalism categories. The winner is announced in April.
www.pulitzer.org

FICTION WINNERS

2006   *March* · Geraldine Brooks

2005   *Gilead* · Marilynne Robinson

2004   *The Known World* · Edward P Jones

2003   *Middlesex* · Jeffrey Eugenides

2002   *Empire Falls* · Richard Russo

2001   *The Amazing Adventures of*
        Kavalier & Clay · Michael Chabon

2000   *Interpreter of Maladies* · Jhumpa Lahiri

1999   *The Hours* · Michael Cunningham

1998   *American Pastoral* · Philip Roth

1997   *Martin Dressler: The Tale of*
        an American Dreamer · Steven Millhauser

1996   *Independence Day* · Richard Ford

1995   *The Stone Diaries* · Carol Shields

NON-FICTION WINNERS

2006   *Imperial Reckoning: The Untold Story of*
        Britain's Gulag in Kenya · Caroline Elkins

6

NATIONAL BOOK AWARDS

Set up in 1950 to bring reading to a wider range of the American public, the winners in the four categories of fiction, poetry, non-fiction and young people's fiction are named in November at a gala ceremony in New York. www.nationalbook.org

FICTION WINNERS

2005	*Europe Central* ·	William T Vollmann
2004	*The News from Paraguay* ·	Lily Tuck
2003	*The Great Fire* ·	Shirley Hazzard
2002	*Three Junes* ·	Julia Glass
2001	*The Corrections* ·	Jonathan Franzen
2000	*In America* ·	Susan Sontag
1999	*Waiting* ·	Ha Jin
1998	*Charming Billy* ·	Alice McDermott
1997	*Cold Mountain* ·	Charles Frazier
1996	*Ship Fever and Other Stories* ·	Andrea Barrett
1995	*Sabbath's Theater* ·	Philip Roth

GOVERNOR GENERAL'S LITERARY AWARDS

Awarded annually to the best English or French language novel, nominations must have been written, translated or illustrated by a Canadian citizen. Winners are announced in November.
http://www.canadacouncil.ca/prizes/ggla

WINNERS

2005   *A Perfect Night to Go to China* · David Gilmour

2004   *A Complicated Kindness* · Miriam Toews

2003   *Elle* · Douglas Glover

2002   *A Song for Nettie Johnson* · Gloria Sawai

2001   *Clara Callan* · Richard B Wright

2000   *Anil's Ghost* · Michael Ondaatje

1999   *Elizabeth and After* · Matt Cohen

1998   *Forms of Devotion* · Diane Schoemperlen

1997   *The Underpainter* · Jane Urquhart

1996   *The Englishman's Boy* · Guy Vanderhaeghe

1995   *The Roaring Girl* · Greg Hollingshead

SCOTIABANK GILLER PRIZE

The Giller, Canada's largest literary award, was set up in 1994 by Toronto businessman Jack Rabinovitch in memory of his late wife, literary journalist Doris Giller. The prize is awarded to the best novel or short story collection published in English by a Canadian citizen.
www.scotiabankgillerprize.ca

WINNERS

2004	*Runaway* · Alice Munro
2003	*The In-Between World of Vikram Lall* · MG Vassanji
2002	*The Polished Hoe* · Austin Clarke
2001	*Clara Callan* · Richard B Wright
2000	*Anil's Ghost* · Michael Ondaatje
2000	*Mercy Among The Children* · David Adams Richards
1999	*A Good House* · Bonnie Burnard
1998	*The Love of a Good Woman* · Alice Munro
1997	*Barney's Version* · Mordecai Richler
1996	*Alias Grace* · Margaret Atwood
1995	*A Fine Balance* · Rohinton Mistry

MILES FRANKLIN AWARDS

Set up at the bequest of author Miles Franklin, this Australian prize rewards the country's leading novelists. Nominees must represent Australia in their work. The winner is announced in June.
www.trust.com.au

WINNERS

2005   *The White Earth* · Andrew McGahan

2004   *The Great Fire* · Shirley Hazzard

2003   *The Journey to the Stone Country* · Alex Miller

2002   *Dirt Music* · Tim Winton

2001   *The Dark Palace* · Frank Moorhouse

2000   *Drylands* · Thea Astley

2000   *Benang* · Kim Scott

1999   *Eucalyptus* · Murray Bail

1998   *Jack Maggs* · Peter Carey

1997   *The Glade within the Grove* · David Foster

1996   *Highways to a War* · Christopher Koch

1995   *The Hand That Signed the Paper* · Helen Demidenko

MONTANA NATIONAL BOOK AWARDS

An amalgamation of the Montana and New Zealand Book Awards, this prize is awarded to the best novel written by a New Zealander in English or Maori. Winners are announced in July.
www.booksellers.co.nz

WINNERS

SUNDAY TIMES ALAN PATON AWARD

This South African award for non-fiction has been awarded since 1989. Entries must be written in English by a South African citizen. www.sundaytimes.co.za

WINNERS

2006	*Aid Safari* · Adam Levin
2006	*Witness to Aids* · Edwin Cameron
2005	*The Number* · Jonny Steinberg
2004	*A Human Being Died That Night* · Pumla Gobodo-Madikizela
2003	*Midlands* · Jonny Steinberg
2002	*The Dressing Station* · Jonathan Kaplan
2001	*A Mouthful of Glass* · Henk van Woerden
2000	*Mandela: The Authorised Biography* · Anthony Sampson
1999	*Country of My Skull* · Antjie Krog and Bram Fischer
1999	*Afrikaner Revolutionary* · Stephen Clingman
1998	*Africa: A Biography of a Continent* · John Reader
1997	*The Seed is Mine* · Charles van Onselen
1996	*The Calling of Katie Makanya* · Margaret McCord
1995	*Long Walk to Freedom* · Nelson Mandela

COMMONWEALTH WRITERS PRIZE

The Commonwealth Writers Prize, established in 1987, is sponsored by the Commonwealth Foundation. Any work of prose fiction is eligible and must have been written by a citizen of the Commonwealth in English. Winners are announced in March.
www.commonwealthwriters.com

WINNERS

2006   *The Secret River* · Kate Grenville

2005   *Small Island* · Andrea Levy

2004   *A Distant Shore* · Caryl Phillips

2003   *The Polished Hoe* · Austin Clarke

2002   *Gould's Book of Fish* · Richard Flanagan

2001   *True History of the Kelly Gang* · Peter Carey

2000   *Disgrace* · J M Coetzee

1999   *Eucalyptus* · Murray Bail

1998   *Jack Maggs* · Peter Carey

1997   *Salt* · Earl Lovelace

1996   *A Fine Balance* · Rohinton Mistry

1995   *Captain Corelli's Mandolin* · Louis de Bernières

INTERNATIONAL IMPAC DUBLIN
LITERARY AWARD

The biggest of the international prizes, this is open to books written in any language and is judged by a panel of international members of the arts world. Nominations are made by public libraries worldwide and the winner is announced in June.
www.impacdublinaward.ie

WINNERS

2006	*The Master* · Colm Tóibín
2005	*The Known World* · Edward P Jones
2004	*This Blinding Absence of Light* · Tahar Ben Jelloun (translated from the French by Linda Coverdale)
2003	*My Name is Red* · Orhan Pamuk (translated from the Turkish by Erdag M. Göknar)
2002	*Atomised* · Michel Houellebecq (translated from the French by Frank Wynne)
2001	*No Great Mischief* · Alistair MacLeod
2000	*Wide Open* · Nicola Barker
1999	*Ingenious Pain* · Andrew Miller
1998	*The Land of Green Plums* · Herta Müller (translated from the German by Michael Hofmann)
1997	*A Heart So White* · Javier Marias (translated from the Spanish by Margaret Jull Costa)
1996	*Remembering Babylon* · David Malouf

LITERARY FESTIVALS

UK

EDINBURGH INTERNATIONAL BOOK FESTIVAL
August is festival time in Edinburgh and the Book Festival is a growing part of its appeal. With over 650 events ranging from readings to debates during the middle two weeks of August there's plenty to interest the book lover. The children's events are also worth a look.
www.edbookfest.co.uk

THE HAY FESTIVAL
This international literature event is based in the Welsh town of Hay-on-Wye, a literary Mecca which boasts 41 bookshops for a population of only 1500. The festival includes a huge range of readings from leading authors, debates, and even a circus. It takes place at the end of May.
www.hayfestival.com

THE CHELTENHAM LITERATURE FESTIVAL
The oldest literature festival in the world, this has been running since 1949 and takes place every October in the spa town of Cheltenham. A ten-day festival, it draws speakers from all over the world and encompasses not only fiction but also poetry, comedy and politics.
www.cheltenhamfestivals.com

PORT ELIOT LIT FEST
The quirkiest of the British festivals, this arts extravaganza takes place in the grounds of Port Eliot, a stately home in Devon. Small but perfectly

formed, it runs over a weekend in mid July and in the past has included burlesque shows, live bands, as well as literary heavyweights.
www.porteliotlitfest.com

NORTH AND SOUTH AMERICA

LOS ANGELES FESTIVAL OF BOOKS

University of California at Los Angeles (UCLA) plays host to over 350 international authors over a weekend each April. They take part in a wide variety of readings and panel discussions. The *Los Angeles Times*-sponsored festival is free, although indoor events do need to be booked.
www.latimes.com/extras/festivalofbooks

MIAMI BOOK FAIR INTERNATIONAL

Originally set up as a two-day street fair, this festival has grown into a week-long event which includes readings.
www.miamibookfair.com

INTERNATIONAL FESTIVAL OF AUTHORS

For eleven days in October Toronto's Waterfront Centre is the host to Canada's largest book event, which includes readings from over 80 international authors. Although not strictly part of the festival, readings also take place every Wednesday at the centre and draw some of the world's most respected authors including Jay McInerney and Peter Carey.
www.readings.org

VANCOUVER INTERNATIONAL
WRITERS & READERS FESTIVAL

Running since 1988, this festival takes place over six days in October and includes readings, debates and seminars for aspiring writers.
www.writersfest.bc.ca

PARATI LITERARY FESTIVAL

A new date on the literary festival itinerary, Parati Literary Festival, or Festa Literaria Internacional de Parati (FLIP) as it's known to the locals, is Brazil's answer to Hay-on-Wye. The pretty seaside port, 300 km south of Rio, is host to readings and book signings, as well as film screenings and music, all staged in tents along the quayside every July.
www.flip.org.br

CARTAGENA DE INDIAS

Set against the beautiful backdrop of Colombia's Caribbean coast, this is a book event with a difference. Organised under the umbrella of the UK's Hay Festival, it is a celebration of Latin American writing and is supported by leading writers such as Carlos Fuentes and Gabriel García Márquez.
www.hayfestival.com/cartagena

AUSTRALIA AND NEW ZEALAND

THE *AGE* MELBOURNE WRITERS FESTIVAL

Drawing writers from all over the globe as well as the best of Australian talent, this is the country's leading literary event. The festival takes place over ten days in mid August.
www.mwf.com.au

ADELAIDE LITERARY FESTIVAL

This seven-day book fiesta in March consists of readings, lectures and 'meet the author' events, many of which take place in the stunning Pioneer Women's Memorial Garden.
www.adelaidefestival.com.au

SYDNEY WRITERS FESTIVAL

With a good mix of academic discussion and lighter readings, the Sydney Writers Festival offers something for every book lover. Held over a week every May in and around Sydney (the stunning blue mountains have been

the location for some readings), the 2006 festival featured writers from over 70 countries.
www.swf.org.au

NEW ZEALAND POST WRITERS AND READERS WEEK
New Zealand's longest-running book event takes place every other May (even years) in Wellington. It's a key event in the three-week-long Arts Festival and draws an international mix of authors including Annie Proulx, Doris Lessing and Arundhati Roy.
www.nzfestival.telecom.co.nz

AUCKLAND WRITERS AND READERS FESTIVAL
This biennial festival, which takes place in May, is a week-long programme of readings, workshops and literary events. It aims to raise the profile of New Zealand authors, as well as offering talks and readings from international authors such as Sarah Waters and Jane Smiley.
www.writersfestival.co.nz

ASIA

UBUD WRITERS AND READERS FESTIVAL
Set in one of Indonesia's most important cultural centres, Bali's Ubud Writers and Readers Festival takes place over four days in October. The Festival includes workshops for aspiring writers, as well as readings, literary lunches and discussions.
www.ubudwritersfestival.com

SINGAPORE WRITERS FESTIVAL
This festival aims to make reading more accessible, and runs for 10 days in late August. It includes screenings and performances, as well as readings. Recent additions to the programme have included discussions about science fiction and fantasy, crime and graphic novels.
www.swf.sg

GREAT READS

AMY TAN

Amy Tan is the author of *The Joy Luck Club*, *The Kitchen God's Wife*, *The Hundred Secret Senses*, *The Bonesetter's Daughter*, *The Opposite of Fate* and *Saving Fish from Drowning*, as well as two children's books, *The Moon Lady* and *The Chinese Siamese Cat*. Her work has been translated into more than thirty-six languages. She lives with her husband in San Francisco and New York.

RECOMMENDED READS

Lolita · Vladimir Nabokov

Jane Eyre · Charlotte Brontë

Love Medicine · Louise Erdrich

Annie John · Jamaica Kincaid

Love in the Time of Cholera · Gabriel García Márquez

The Canterbury Tales · Chaucer

Alice in Wonderland · Lewis Carroll

Psychopathia Sexualis · Richard von Krafft-Ebing

Speak, Memory · Vladimir Nabokov

ANNIE PROULX

Annie Proulx lives in Wyoming. She published her first novel, *Postcards,* in 1991 at the age of 56. Her second novel, *The Shipping News*, won the *Irish Times* International Prize, the Pulitzer Prize and the National Book Award. Her third novel, *Accordion Crimes*, was published in 1996 and her fifth novel, *That Old Ace in the Hole*, in 2003. She is the author of three short story collections:

Heart Songs, *Bad Dirt* and *Close Range*, which includes 'Brokeback Mountain', recently adapted into the award-winning film.

RECOMMENDED READS
The Weather Makers · Tim Flannery
The Clearing · Tim Gautreaux
The Ordinary Seaman/The Divine Husband ·
   Francisco Goldman
Little Infamies/The Maze · Panos Karnezis
The Rabbiter's Bounty · Les Murray
Eating Stone · Ellen Meloy
Goya · Robert Hughes
Tooth and Claw · T C Boyle
Drown · Junot Diaz
Hateship, Friendship, Courtship, Marriage/
   Dance of the Happy Shades · Alice Munro

CHIMAMANDA NGOZI ADICHIE

Chimamanda Ngozi Adichie was born in Nigeria in 1977. She is from Abba, in Anambra State, but grew up in the university town of Nsukka. She went on to receive a BS in Communication and Political Science from Eastern Connecticut State University and an MA from Johns Hopkins University, both in the United States. Her short fiction has been published in literary journals including *Granta*, and won the International PEN/David Wong award in 2003. *Purple Hibiscus*, her first novel, was shortlisted for the Orange Prize and the John Llewellyn Rhys Prize and was winner of the Hurston/Wright Legacy award for debut fiction. She was a Hodder fellow at Princeton University for the 2005–2006 academic year. She lives in Nigeria.

RECOMMENDED READS
Arrow of God · Chinua Achebe
The Time of our Singing · Richard Powers

No Sweetness Here · Ama Ata Aidoo
Harvest of Thorns · Shimmer Chinodya
Woman at Point Zero · Nawal El Saadawi
The Beautyful Ones Are Not Yet Born · Ayi Kwei Armah
Reef · Romesh Gunesekera
The Bluest Eye · Toni Morrison
Reading in the Dark · Seamus Deane
A Strange and Sublime Address · Amit Chaudhuri

CONN IGGULDEN

Born in the UK, Conn Iggulden read English at London University and worked as a teacher for seven years before becoming a full-time writer. He lives in Hertfordshire with his wife and children. Conn Iggulden is the author of the number one bestselling Emperor series, *Blackwater*, and co-author of *The Dangerous Book for Boys*.

RECOMMENDED READS
Patrick O'Brian's novels
Bernard Cornwell's novels
The Flashman Series · George MacDonald Fraser
Tai Pan · James Clavell
The Courtney Series · Wilbur Smith
The Hornblower books · C S Forester
The Night's Dawn trilogy · Peter F Hamilton
The Liveship Traders Series · Robin Hobb
Cujo/The Dead Zone · Stephen King
The Seafort Saga · David Feintuch

FRANK McCOURT

Frank McCourt is the author of *Angela's Ashes*, which won the 1997 Pulitzer Prize, the National Book Critics' Circle Award, the *Los Angeles Times* Award and the Royal Society of Literature Award amongst others, and rapidly became a bestseller, topping all charts worldwide for over three years. *'Tis* and *Teacher Man,* the sequels, continued their predecessor's huge success and the books have been published in more than twenty countries and languages. He lives in Connecticut and New York.

RECOMMENDED READS

The Adventures of Huckleberry Finn · Mark Twain
The Magic Mountain · Thomas Mann
The Seven Storey Mountain · Thomas Merton
The Life of Saint Teresa of Ávila by Herself
The Code of the Woosters · P G Wodehouse
Birdsong · Sebastian Faulks
A Long Long Way · Sebastian Barry
The Dark · John McGahern
Tristram Shandy · Laurence Sterne
Pride and Prejudice · Jane Austen

ISABEL ALLENDE

Isabel Allende was born in 1942, the niece of Salvador Allende, the elected President of Chile deposed in a CIA-backed coup in 1973. She worked as a journalist, playwright and children's writer in Chile until 1974 and then in Venezuela until 1987. Her first novel for adults, *The House of the Spirits,* was published in Spanish in 1982. It was an international sensation, and ever since all her books have been acclaimed and adored in numerous translations world-wide. In 1987 she married an American and became an immigrant to the United States, where she has written most of her books.

RECOMMENDED READS

Poetry · Pablo Neruda
One Hundred Years of Solitude · Gabriel García Márquez
The Female Eunuch · Germaine Greer
The Ascent of Man · Jacob Bronowski

The Aleph · Jorge Luis Borges
The Tin Drum · Günter Grass
War and Peace · Leo Tolstoy
Memoirs of Hadrian · Marguerite Yourcenar
A Thousand and One Nights
Aunt Julia and the Scriptwriter · Mario Vargas Llosa

J G BALLARD

J G Ballard was born in 1930 in Shanghai, China. Following the attack on Pearl Harbor, Ballard and his family were placed in a civilian prison camp, returning to England in 1946. After two years at Cambridge, where he read medicine, Ballard worked as a copywriter and Covent Garden porter before going to Canada with the RAF. He started writing short stories in the late 1950s, while working on a scientific journal. His first major novel, *The Drowned World*, was published in 1962. His acclaimed novels include *The Crystal World*, *The Atrocity Exhibition*, *Crash* (filmed by David Cronenberg), *High-Rise*, *The Unlimited Dream Company*, *The Kindness of Women* (the sequel to *Empire of the Sun*), *Cocaine Nights*, *Super-Cannes*, *Millennium People* and, most recently, *Kingdom Come*.

RECOMMENDED READS

Moby-Dick · Herman Melville
The Loved One · Evelyn Waugh
The Big Sleep · Raymond Chandler
Alice's Adventures in Wonderland · Lewis Carroll
The Trial · Franz Kafka
The Tempest · William Shakespeare
Catch-22 · Joseph Heller
Our Man in Havana · Graham Greene
1984 · George Orwell
Brave New World · Aldous Huxley

JOYCE CAROL OATES

Joyce Carol Oates is the recipient of the National Book Award, the PEN/Malamud Award for Excellence in Short Fiction and the Prix Femina. She has written some of the most enduring fiction of our time, including *We Were the Mulvaneys*, which was an Oprah Book Club Choice, and *Blonde*, which was nominated for the National Book Award. She is the Roger S Berlind Distinguished Professor of Humanities at Princeton University.

RECOMMENDED READS

The Collected Poems of Emily Dickinson
Ulysses · James Joyce
Moby-Dick · Herman Melville
Walden · Henry David Thoreau
Madame Bovary · Gustave Flaubert
The Sound and the Fury · William Faulkner
The Odyssey · Homer (translated by Robert Fagles)
The Turn of the Screw · Henry James
Collected Stories of Franz Kafka
King Lear · Shakespeare
Collected Stories of D H Lawrence

SIMON SINGH

Simon Singh received his PhD in particle physics from the University of Cambridge. A former BBC producer, he directed the BAFTA award-winning documentary film *Fermat's Last Theorem* and wrote the bestselling book of the same name, followed by *The Code Book*, also a bestseller. His latest book is *Big Bang*, a fascinating exploration of the question of how our universe was created.

RECOMMENDED READS

Surely You're Joking, Mr Feynman! · Richard P Feynman
The Making of the Atomic Bomb · Richard Rhodes
Chaos · James Gleick

Flatland · Edwin A. Abbott
A Mathematician's Apology · G H Hardy
Our Final Century · Martin Rees
The Surgeon of Crowthorne · Simon Winchester
Dr Tatiana's Sex Advice to All Creation · Olivia Judson
Interpreter of Maladies · Jhumpa Lahiri
The Phantom Tollbooth · Norton Juster

TASH AW

Tash Aw grew up in Malaysia and moved to England at the age of 18 to attend university. His first novel, *The Harmony Silk Factory*, won the 2005 Whitbread First Novel Award and the Commonwealth Writers Prize (Asia Pacific Region), and was also nominated for the MAN Booker Prize and *Guardian* First Novel Prize. It is currently being translated into 18 languages. He lives in London where he is at work on his second novel.

RECOMMENDED READS
The Sound and the Fury · William Faulkner
Moby-Dick · Herman Melville
Earthly Powers · Anthony Burgess
Haunts of the Black Masseur: The Swimmer as Hero ·
   Charles Sprawson
East of Eden · John Steinbeck
Anna Karenina · Leo Tolstoy
Lord Jim · Joseph Conrad
In Patagonia · Bruce Chatwin
Trois Contes · Gustave Flaubert
Lolita · Vladimir Nabokov

10 STEPS TO SETTING UP
A READING GROUP

- Find a group of like-minded individuals. Ask friends or friends of friends, look for an established group looking for new members or set up your own. Local libraries and bookshops are often good sources of information on existing groups.

- The ideal reading group size is around eight members – too few and it can be hard to get a discussion started.

- If you're starting a new group you'll need to decide how often you want to meet up. A monthly arrangement seems to work well for most as it gives everyone a chance to read the chosen book, no matter how slow a reader.

- Try to find a quiet place to meet. Pubs without loud background noise, cafés and members' homes work well.

- Letting each member of the group pick a book in turn means you should have the opportunity to read a wide range of authors and will hopefully be introduced to some new ones.

- For inspiration as to which books to pick, look at newspaper book sections or the lists of prize winners in this journal.

- A reading group can be as formal or relaxed as its members want it to be. For more formal groups, a pre-prepared list of questions about the book keeps the discussion moving forward. Check publishers' websites, as they now often offer reading guides to the books they publish, or search the internet for more information about your chosen book and author. More informal groups may find it sufficient to let the person who chose the book give their opinion first and let the discussion develop from there.

- If you're finding it hard to get a discussion going, a simple question about what each member liked and disliked about the book can bring up some topics to think about. Other aspects to think about include character and location and their authenticity, plot development, the central themes of the book and the way it is written.

- Sticking post-it notes next to sections of the book that interest you as you read can help you remember points that you were interested in.

- For more information visit www.readinggroups.co.uk, www.newbooks mag.com or www.bookgroup.info or try the following guides: *Reading Groups* by Jenny Hartley (Oxford University Press); *The Essential Guide for Reading Groups* by Susan Osborne (Bloomsbury); *The Good Reading Guide: What to Read and What to Read Next*, edited by Nick Rennison (Bloomsbury).

NOTES

A

TITLE _Brooklyn Follies_

AUTHOR _AUSTER PAUL_

DATE _20 July 08_

COMMENTS - American. Well written — enjoyable at first
Nathan e Tom — Lucy arrives — look for mother — married to
religious bigot. (Church Book Sale)

TITLE _____

AUTHOR _____

DATE _____

COMMENTS

'Time is a blind guide.' ∾ *Fugitive Pieces* ANNE MICHAELS

TITLE _J. A. 3._

AUTHOR _Nahlio Jenner   - sept 2020_

DATE _____

COMMENTS _From Scotsman Mag._

TITLE _____

AUTHOR __Hannah_____Rohnfeld__

DATE _____ May 2020

COMMENTS   from   Endy.

I'm probability a Leda
House of Twlumy

'It was a bright cold day in April, and the clocks were striking thirteen.'
1984 GEORGE ORWELL

TITLE _100 Summus_

AUTHOR _Vaness Branson_

DATE _May 20__

COMMENTS _Funn Lady._

'They shoot the white girl first.' ∾ *Paradise* TONI MORRISON

TITLE _____

AUTHOR _____

DATE _____

COMMENTS

'It was a queer, sultry summer, the summer they electrocuted the Rosenbergs, and I didn't know what I was doing in New York.' ∾ *The Bell Jar* SYLVIA PLATH

TITLE _____

AUTHOR _____

DATE _____

COMMENTS

'The sweat wis lashing oafay Sick Boy; he is trembling.' ∾ *Trainspotting* IRVINE WELSH

TITLE _____

AUTHOR _____

DATE _____

COMMENTS

'When the lights went off the accompanist kissed her.' ∾ *Bel Canto* ANN PATCHETT

Reading Group

TITLE _____

AUTHOR _____

DATE _____

COMMENTS

'"Christmas isn't Christmas without any presents," grumbled Jo, lying on the rug.'
Little Women LOUISA MAY ALCOTT

TITLE _____

AUTHOR _____

DATE _____

COMMENTS

'The great fish moved silently through the night water, propelled by short sweeps of its crescent tail.' ∽ *Jaws* PETER BENCHLEY

TITLE _____

AUTHOR _____

DATE _____

COMMENTS

'Lolita, light of my life, fire of my loins.' ∞ *Lolita* VLADIMIR NABOKOV

TITLE _____

AUTHOR _____

DATE _____

COMMENTS

'I was born twice: first, as a baby girl, on a remarkably smogless Detroit day in January of 1960; and then again, as a teenage boy, in an emergency room near Petoskey, Michigan, in August of 1974.' ❧ *Middlesex* JEFFREY EUGENIDES

TITLE _____

AUTHOR _____

DATE _____

COMMENTS

'Mrs Dalloway said she would buy the flowers herself.'
Mrs Dalloway VIRGINIA WOOLF

TITLE _____

AUTHOR _____

DATE _____

COMMENTS

'My name was Salmon, like the fish; first name Susie. I was fourteen when I was murdered on December 6, 1973.' ∾ *The Lovely Bones* ALICE SEBOLD

Reading Group ✓

TITLE _____

AUTHOR _____

DATE _____

COMMENTS

'Happy families are all alike; every unhappy family is unhappy in its own way.'
Anna Karenina LEO TOLSTOY

TITLE _____

AUTHOR _____

DATE _____

COMMENTS

'Once upon a time, there was a woman who discovered she had turned into the wrong person.' ∾ *Back When We Were Grownups* ANNE TYLER ✓ Own Choice

TITLE _____

AUTHOR _____

DATE _____

COMMENTS

'You better not never tell nobody but God.' ❧ *The Color Purple* ALICE WALKER

'The past is a foreign country; they do things differently there.'
The Go-Between L P HARTLEY

TITLE _____

AUTHOR _____

DATE _____

COMMENTS

'Vaughan died yesterday in his last car-crash.' ❧ *Crash* J G BALLARD

TITLE _____

AUTHOR _____

DATE _____

COMMENTS

'In the town, there were two mutes and they were always together.'
The Heart is a Lonely Hunter CARSON McCULLERS

TITLE _____

AUTHOR _____

DATE _____

COMMENTS

'Nothing to me is so erotic as a hotel room, and therefore so penetrated with life and death.'
Hotel Honolulu PAUL THEROUX

TITLE _____

AUTHOR _____

DATE _____

COMMENTS

'To begin at the beginning: It is spring, moonless night in the small town, starless and bible-black.' ∞ *Under Milk Wood* DYLAN THOMAS

TITLE _____

AUTHOR _____

DATE _____

COMMENTS

'When he was nearly thirteen, my brother Jem got his arm badly broken at the elbow.'
To Kill a Mockingbird HARPER LEE

TITLE _____

AUTHOR _____

DATE _____

COMMENTS

'Far out in the uncharted backwaters of the unfashionable end of the Western Spiral arm
of the Galaxy lies a small unregarded yellow sun.'
The Hitchhiker's Guide to the Galaxy DOUGLAS ADAMS

TITLE _____

AUTHOR _____

DATE _____

COMMENTS

'I write this sitting in the kitchen sink.' ∾ *I Capture the Castle* DODIE SMITH

TITLE _____

AUTHOR _____

DATE _____

COMMENTS

'Dr Iannis had enjoyed a satisfactory day in which none of his patients had died or got any worse.' ❧ *Captain Corelli's Mandolin* LOUIS DE BERNIÈRES

TITLE _____

AUTHOR _____

DATE _____

COMMENTS

TITLE _____

AUTHOR _____

DATE _____

COMMENTS

'The blow was such a stunner that it was thirteen years before I could get back on my feet again.' ∾ *Papillon* HENRI CHARRIÈRE

TITLE _____

AUTHOR _____

DATE _____

COMMENTS

TITLE _____

AUTHOR _____

DATE _____

COMMENTS

'"To be born again," sang Gibreel Farishta tumbling from the heavens, "first you have to die." ∾ *The Satanic Verses* SALMAN RUSHDIE

TITLE _____

AUTHOR _____

DATE _____

COMMENTS

'Things started to fall apart at home when my brother, Jaja, did not go to communion
and Papa flung his heavy missal across the room and broke the figurines on the étagère.'
Purple Hibiscus CHIMAMANDA NGOZI ADICHIE

own choice
e Reading Gp.

TITLE _____

AUTHOR _____

DATE _____

COMMENTS

'I first met Dean not long after my wife and I split up.' ∽ *On the Road* JACK KEROUAC

TITLE _____

AUTHOR _____

DATE _____

COMMENTS

'May in Ayemenem is a hot, brooding month. The days are long and humid.
The river shrinks and black crows gorge on bright mangoes in still, dustgreen trees.'
The God of Small Things ARUNDHATI ROY

TITLE _____

AUTHOR _____

DATE _____

COMMENTS

'Amerigo Bonasera sat in New York Criminal Court Number 3 and waited for justice;
vengeance on the men who had so cruelly hurt his daughter, who had tried to dishonor
her.' ∾ *The Godfather* MARIO PUZO

TITLE _____

AUTHOR _____

DATE _____

COMMENTS

'I will not drink more than fourteen alcohol units a week.'
Bridget Jones's Diary HELEN FIELDING

✓ own choice

rubbish !

TITLE _____

AUTHOR _____

DATE _____

COMMENTS

'I was born in 1927, the only child of middle-class parents, both English, and themselves
born in the grotesquely elongated shadow, which they never rose sufficiently above history
to leave, of that monstrous dwarf Queen Victoria.' ❧ *The Magus* JOHN FOWLES

TITLE _____

AUTHOR _____

DATE _____

COMMENTS

'We started dying before the snow, and like the snow, we continued to fall.'
Tracks LOUISE ERDRICH

TITLE _____

AUTHOR _____

DATE _____

COMMENTS

'One evening in the spring of 1936, when I was a boy of fourteen, my father took me to a dance performance in Kyoto. I remember only two things about it.'
Memoirs of a Geisha ARTHUR S GOLDEN

TITLE _____

AUTHOR _____

DATE _____

COMMENTS

'The summer she was fifteen, Melanie discovered she was made of flesh and blood.'
The Magic Toyshop ANGELA CARTER

TITLE _____

AUTHOR _____

DATE _____

COMMENTS

'On an exceptionally hot evening early in July, a young man came out of the garret in which he lodged in S. Place and walked slowly, as though in hesitation, towards K. bridge.'
Crime and Punishment FYODOR DOSTOYEVSKY

TITLE _____

AUTHOR _____

DATE _____

COMMENTS

'Ennis del Mar wakes before five, wind rocking the trailer, hissing in around the aluminium door and window frames.' ❧ *Brokeback Mountain* ANNIE PROULX

TITLE _____

AUTHOR _____

DATE _____

COMMENTS

'The first place that I can well remember was a large pleasant meadow with a pond of clear water in it.' ∽ *Black Beauty* ANNA SEWELL

TITLE _____

AUTHOR _____

DATE _____

COMMENTS

TITLE _____

AUTHOR _____

DATE _____

COMMENTS

'The terror, which would not end for another twenty-eight years if it ever did end began, so far as I know or can tell, with a boat made from a sheet of newspaper floating down a gutter swollen with rain.' ∾ *It* STEPHEN KING

TITLE _____

AUTHOR _____

DATE _____

COMMENTS

'In his ex-wife's clever decorating magazines Douglas Cheeseman had seen mattress ticking being amusing.' ∾ *The Idea of Perfection* KATE GRENVILLE

own choice e Reading Group

TITLE _____

AUTHOR _____

DATE _____

COMMENTS

'To the red country and part of the gray country of Oklahoma, the last rains came gently, and they did not cut the scarred earth.' ❧ *The Grapes of Wrath* JOHN STEINBECK

TITLE _____

AUTHOR _____

DATE _____

COMMENTS

'Through the frayed curtain at my window a wan glow announces the break of day.'
The Diving-Bell and the Butterfly JEAN-DOMINIQUE BAUBY

TITLE _____

AUTHOR _____

DATE _____

COMMENTS

'Scarlett O'Hara was not beautiful, but men seldom realized it when caught by her charm as the Tarleton twins were.' ∾ *Gone With the Wind* MARGARET MITCHELL

TITLE _____

AUTHOR _____

DATE _____

COMMENTS

'Mr. Utterson the lawyer was a man of a rugged countenance, that was never lighted by a smile; cold, scanty and embarrassed in discourse; backward in sentiment; lean, long, dusty, dreary, and yet somehow lovable.'
The Strange Case of Dr Jekyll and Mr Hyde ROBERT LOUIS STEVENSON

TITLE _____

AUTHOR _____

DATE _____

COMMENTS

'In my younger and more vulnerable years my father gave me some advice that I've been turning over in my mind ever since.' ❧ *The Great Gatsby* F SCOTT FITZGERALD

Own Choice

TITLE _____

AUTHOR _____

DATE _____

COMMENTS

.

TITLE _____

AUTHOR _____

DATE _____

COMMENTS

TITLE _____

AUTHOR _____

DATE _____

COMMENTS

'Garp's mother, Jenny Fields, was arrested in Boston in 1942 for wounding a man in a movie theatre.' ∾ *The World According to Garp* JOHN IRVING

TITLE _____

AUTHOR _____

DATE _____

COMMENTS

'One thing was certain, that the white kitten had had nothing to do with it, it was the black kitten's fault entirely.' ∾ *Through the Looking Glass* LEWIS CARROLL

As a child

TITLE _____

AUTHOR _____

DATE _____

COMMENTS

'My name is Elizabeth but no one's ever called me that.' ∾ *How I Live Now* MEG ROSOFF

TITLE _____

AUTHOR _____

DATE _____

COMMENTS

'"I have been here before," I said; I had been there before; first with Sebastian more
than twenty years ago on a cloudless day in June, when the ditches were creamy with
meadowsweet and the air heavy with all the scents of summer.'
Brideshead Revisited EVELYN WAUGH

TITLE _____

AUTHOR _____

DATE _____

COMMENTS

'By dawn at least half the members of the Kelly gang were badly wounded and it was then the creature appeared from behind police lines.'
True History of the Kelly Gang PETER CAREY

TITLE _____

AUTHOR _____

DATE _____

COMMENTS

'It was in the citadel of Feroz Shah Kotla that I met my first Sufi.'
City of Djinns WILLIAM DALRYMPLE

TITLE _____

AUTHOR _____

DATE _____

COMMENTS

_____

'Mr. and Mrs Dursley, of number four, Privet Drive, were proud to say that they were
perfectly normal, thank you very much.'
Harry Potter and the Sorcerer's Stone J K ROWLING

'At sixty miles per hour, you could pass our farm in a minute, on County Road 686, which ran due north into the T intersection at Cabot Street Road.'
A Thousand Acres JANE SMILEY

TITLE _____

AUTHOR _____

DATE _____

COMMENTS

TITLE _____

AUTHOR _____

DATE _____

COMMENTS

TITLE _____

AUTHOR _____

DATE _____

COMMENTS

own choice

great !

TITLE _____

AUTHOR _____

DATE _____

COMMENTS

'All this happened, more or less.' ∾ *Slaughterhouse-Five* KURT VONNEGUT

TITLE _____

AUTHOR _____

DATE _____

COMMENTS

"'The Signora had no business to do it," said Miss Bartlett, "no business at all.'"
A Room with a View E M FORSTER

TITLE _____

AUTHOR _____

DATE _____

COMMENTS

TITLE _____

AUTHOR _____

DATE _____

COMMENTS

'Under certain circumstances there are few hours in life more agreeable than the hour dedicated to the ceremony known as afternoon tea.'
The Portrait of a Lady HENRY JAMES

TITLE _____

AUTHOR _____

DATE _____

COMMENTS

'Beyond the Indian hamlet, upon a forlorn strand, I happened on a trail of recent footprints.' ∽ *Cloud Atlas* DAVID MITCHELL

TITLE _____

AUTHOR _____

DATE _____

COMMENTS

'Everyone had always said that John would be a preacher when he grew up, just like his father.' ∾ *Go Tell It on the Mountain* JAMES BALDWIN

TITLE _____

AUTHOR _____

DATE _____

COMMENTS

'Grandfather's skirts would flap in the wind along the churchyard path and I would
hang on.' ∾ *Bad Blood* LORNA SAGE

TITLE _____

AUTHOR _____

DATE _____

COMMENTS

'Hale knew, before he had been in Brighton three hours, that they meant to murder him.'
Brighton Rock GRAHAM GREENE

TITLE _____

AUTHOR _____

DATE _____

COMMENTS

'One day, I was already old, in the entrance of a public place a man came up to me.'
The Lover MARGUERITE DURAS

TITLE _____

AUTHOR _____

DATE _____

COMMENTS

TITLE _____

AUTHOR _____

DATE _____

COMMENTS

'The boy with fair hair lowered himself down the last few feet of rock and began to pick his way toward the lagoon.' ❧ *The Lord of the Flies* WILLIAM GOLDING

TITLE _____

AUTHOR _____

DATE _____

COMMENTS

'On white paper my mother has written, *Last night I walked where he had.*'
Eve Green SUSAN FLETCHER

TITLE _____

AUTHOR _____

DATE _____

COMMENTS

'This is a true story but I can't believe it's really happening.'
London Fields MARTIN AMIS

TITLE _____

AUTHOR _____

DATE _____

COMMENTS

'The *Nellie*, a cruising yawl, swung to her anchor without a flutter of the sails, and was at rest.' ∾ *Heart of Darkness* JOSEPH CONRAD

TITLE _____

AUTHOR _____

DATE _____

COMMENTS

'She was so deeply imbedded in my consciousness that for the first year of school I seem to have believed that each of my teachers was my mother in disguise.'
Portnoy's Complaint PHILIP ROTH

TITLE _____

AUTHOR _____

DATE _____

COMMENTS

TITLE _____

AUTHOR _____

DATE _____

COMMENTS

'If you really want to hear about it, the first thing you'll probably want to know is where
I was born, and what my lousy childhood was like . . .'
The Catcher in the Rye J D SALINGER

TITLE _____

AUTHOR _____

DATE _____

COMMENTS

'Ten days after the war ended, my sister Laura drove a car off a bridge.'
The Blind Assassin MARGARET ATWOOD

Couldn't finish it

TITLE _____

AUTHOR _____

DATE _____

COMMENTS

'There are still the flowers to buy.' ∽ *The Hours* MICHAEL CUNNINGHAM

TITLE _____

AUTHOR _____

DATE _____

COMMENTS

'Early in the morning, late in the century, Cricklewood Broadway.'
White Teeth ZADIE SMITH

TITLE _____

AUTHOR _____

DATE _____

COMMENTS

'How death enters your life.' ❧ *Middle Age* JOYCE CAROL OATES

TITLE _____

AUTHOR _____

DATE _____

COMMENTS

'He speaks in your voice, American, and there's a shine in his eyes that's halfway hopeful.'
Underworld DON DELILLO

TITLE _____

AUTHOR _____

DATE _____

COMMENTS

'Dora Greenfield left her husband because she was afraid of him.'
The Bell IRIS MURDOCH

TITLE _____

AUTHOR _____

DATE _____

COMMENTS

'One mid-winter day off the coast of Massachusetts, the crew of a mackerel schooner spotted a bottle with a note in it.' ∽ *The Perfect Storm* SEBASTIAN JUNGER

TITLE _____

AUTHOR _____

DATE _____

COMMENTS

'The sky above the port was the color of television, tuned to a dead channel.'
Neuromancer WILLIAM GIBSON

TITLE _____

AUTHOR _____

DATE _____

COMMENTS

'Mother died today.' ∾ *The Stranger* ALBERT CAMUS

TITLE _____

AUTHOR _____

DATE _____

COMMENTS

'It was about eleven o'clock in the morning, mid October, with the sun not shining and a look of hard wet rain in the clearness of the foothills.'
The Big Sleep RAYMOND CHANDLER

TITLE _____

AUTHOR _____

DATE _____

COMMENTS

'Many years later, as he faced the firing squad, Colonel Aureliano Buendia was to remember that distant afternoon when his father took him to discover ice.'
One Hundred Years of Solitude GABRIEL GARCÍA MÁRQUEZ

TITLE _____

AUTHOR _____

DATE _____

COMMENTS

'Emma Woodhouse, handsome, clever, and rich, with a comfortable home and happy disposition, seemed to unite some of the best blessings of existence; and had lived nearly twenty-one years in the world with very little to distress or vex her.'
Emma JANE AUSTEN

TITLE _____

AUTHOR _____

DATE _____

COMMENTS

'First of all, it was October, a rare month for boys.'
Something Wicked This Way Comes RAY BRADBURY

TITLE _____

AUTHOR _____

DATE _____

COMMENTS

'What came first, the music or the misery?' ∾ *High Fidelity* NICK HORNBY

TITLE _____

AUTHOR _____

DATE _____

COMMENTS

'This is not a story of incredible heroism, or merely the narrative of a cynic; at least I do not mean it to be.' ᐁ *The Motorcycle Diaries* CHE GUEVARA

'They say when trouble comes close ranks, and so the white people did.'
Wide Sargasso Sea JEAN RHYS

TITLE _____

AUTHOR _____

DATE _____

COMMENTS

'My name, in those days, was Susan Trinder.' ❧ *Fingersmith* SARAH WATERS

TITLE _____

AUTHOR _____

DATE _____

COMMENTS

'Odd that mankind's benefactors should be amusing people.'
Ravelstein SAUL BELLOWS

TITLE _____

AUTHOR _____

DATE _____

COMMENTS

'Sidda is a girl again in the hot heart of Louisiana, the bayou world of Catholic saints and voodoo queens.' ∾ *Divine Secrets of the Ya-Ya Sisterhood* REBECCA WELLS

TITLE _____

AUTHOR _____

DATE _____

COMMENTS

'The Harmony Silk Factory is the name of the shophouse my father bought in 1942 as a front for his illegal businesses.' ∾ *The Harmony Silk Factory* TASH AW

TITLE _____

AUTHOR _____

DATE _____

COMMENTS

'When I stepped out into the bright sunlight from the darkness of the movie house, I had only two things on my mind: Paul Newman and a ride home.'
The Outsiders S E HINTON

'Everything starts somewhere, although many physicists disagree.'
Hogfather: A Novel of Discworld TERRY PRATCHETT

TITLE _____

AUTHOR _____

DATE _____

COMMENTS

'Georgette was a hip queer.' ∾ *Last Exit to Brooklyn* HUBERT SELBY JR.

'It was the best of times, it was the worst of times.'
A Tale of Two Cities CHARLES DICKENS

TITLE _____

AUTHOR _____

DATE _____

COMMENTS

'James Bond, with two double bourbons inside him, sat in the final departure lounge of Miami Airport and thought about life and death.' ∿ *Goldfinger* IAN FLEMING

TITLE _____

AUTHOR _____

DATE _____

COMMENTS

TITLE _____

AUTHOR _____

DATE _____

COMMENTS

'Here is Edward Bear, coming downstairs now, bump, bump, bump, on the back of his head, behind Christopher Robin.' ∾ *Winnie the Pooh* A A MILNE

TITLE _____

AUTHOR _____

DATE _____

COMMENTS

'My father and mother should have stayed in New York where they met and married and where I was born.' ∽ *Angela's Ashes* FRANK MCCOURT

TITLE _____

AUTHOR _____

DATE _____

COMMENTS

'It was the day my grandmother exploded.' ∽ *The Crow Road* IAIN M BANKS

TITLE _____

AUTHOR _____

DATE _____

COMMENTS

'The branches are bare, the sky tonight a milky violet.' ∾ *An Equal Music* VIKRAM SETH

TITLE _____

AUTHOR _____

DATE _____

COMMENTS

'Everyone is born with some special talent, and Eliza Sommers discovered early
on that she had two: a good sense of smell and a good memory.'
Daughter of Fortune ISABEL ALLENDE

TITLE _____

AUTHOR _____

DATE _____

COMMENTS

'riverrun, past Eve and Adam's, from swerve of shore to bend of bay, brings us by a commodius vicus of recirculation back to Howth Castle and Environs.'
Finnegans Wake JAMES JOYCE

TITLE _____

AUTHOR _____

DATE _____

COMMENTS

'You will rejoice to hear that no disaster has accompanied the commencement of an enterprise which you have regarded with such evil forebodings.'
Frankenstein MARY SHELLEY

TITLE _____

AUTHOR _____

DATE _____

COMMENTS

'He lay flat on the brown, pine-needled floor of the forest, his chin on his folded arms, and high overhead the wind blew in the tops of the pine trees.'
For Whom the Bell Tolls ERNEST HEMINGWAY

TITLE _____

AUTHOR _____

DATE _____

COMMENTS

'My mother did not tell me they were coming.'
Girl with a Pearl Earring TRACY CHEVALIER

TITLE _____

AUTHOR _____

DATE _____

COMMENTS

'A single line of blood trickles down the pale underside of her arm, a red seam on a white sleeve.' ❧ *Labyrinth* KATE MOSSE

TITLE _____

AUTHOR _____

DATE _____

COMMENTS

'By mistake Larry Weller took someone else's Harris tweed jacket instead of his own, and it wasn't till he jammed his hand in the pocket that he knew something was wrong.'
Larry's Party CAROL SHIELDS

TITLE _____

AUTHOR _____

DATE _____

COMMENTS

'My suffering left me sad and lonely.' ∾ *Life of Pi* YANN MARTEL

TITLE _____

AUTHOR _____

DATE _____

COMMENTS

'My mother called me Silver.' ∾ *Lighthousekeeping* JEANETTE WINTERSON

TITLE _____

AUTHOR _____

DATE _____

COMMENTS

'Once on a Wednesday excursion when I was a little girl, my father bought me a beaded wire ball that I loved.' ∾ *Longitude* DAVA SOBEL

TITLE _____

AUTHOR _____

DATE _____

COMMENTS

'This is what I write to her: *The clouds tonight embossed the sky. A dipping sun gilded and brazed each raveling edge as if the firmament were threaded through with precious filaments.*'
March GERALDINE BROOKS

TITLE _____

AUTHOR _____

DATE _____

COMMENTS

'Death is outside life but it alters it.' ❧ *Miss Garnet's Angel* SALLEY VICKERS ✓

TITLE _____

AUTHOR _____

DATE _____

COMMENTS

TITLE _____

AUTHOR _____

DATE _____

COMMENTS

TITLE _____

AUTHOR _____

DATE _____

COMMENTS

'In the beginning there was a river.' ❧ *The Famished Road* BEN OKRI

TITLE _____

AUTHOR _____

DATE _____

COMMENTS

'Early one spring morning in 1989, I rode my Flying Pigeon bicycle through the streets of Nanjing dreaming about my son PanPan.' ✆ *The Good Women of China* XINRAN

TITLE _____

AUTHOR _____

DATE _____

COMMENTS

TITLE _____

AUTHOR _____

DATE _____

COMMENTS

'Samuel Spade's jaw was long and bony, his chin a jutting v under the more flexible v of his mouth.' ∾ *The Maltese Falcon* DASHIELL HAMMETT

TITLE _____

AUTHOR _____

DATE _____

COMMENTS

'1801 – I have just returned from a visit to my landlord – the solitary neighbour that
I shall be troubled with.' ∾ *Wuthering Heights* EMILY BRONTË

TITLE _____

AUTHOR _____

DATE _____

COMMENTS

'Mrs Lora Delane Porter dismissed the hireling who had brought her automobile around from the garage and seated herself at the wheel.' ❧ *The Coming of Bill* P G WODEHOUSE

TITLE _____

AUTHOR _____

DATE _____

COMMENTS

'Gustave Aschenback – or von Aschenback, as he had been known officially since his fiftieth birthday – had set out alone from his house in Prince Regent Street, Munich, for an extended walk.' ∽ *Death in Venice* THOMAS MANN

TITLE _____

AUTHOR _____

DATE _____

COMMENTS

'We came on the wind of the carnival.' ∾ *Chocolat* JOANNE HARRIS

TITLE _____

AUTHOR _____

DATE _____

COMMENTS

'In eighteenth-century France there lived a man who was one of the most gifted and abominable personages in an era that knew no lack of gifted and abominable personages.'
Perfume PATRICK SÜSKIND

TITLE _____

AUTHOR _____

DATE _____

COMMENTS

'Three hundred and forty-eight years, six months, and nineteen days ago, the good people of Paris awoke to the sound of all the bells pealing in the three districts of the Cité, the Université, and the Ville.' ∽ *The Hunchback of Notre-Dame* VICTOR HUGO

TITLE _____

AUTHOR _____

DATE _____

COMMENTS

'The world is what it is; men who are nothing, who allow themselves to become nothing, have no place in it.' ∾ *A Bend in the River* V S NAIPAUL

TITLE _____

AUTHOR _____

DATE _____

COMMENTS

'The schoolmaster was leaving the village, and everybody seemed sorry.'
Jude the Obscure THOMAS HARDY

TITLE _____

AUTHOR _____

DATE _____

COMMENTS

'CLARE: The library is cool and smells like carpet cleaner, although all I can see is marble.'
The Time Traveler's Wife AUDREY NIFFENEGGER ✓

TITLE _____

AUTHOR _____

DATE _____

COMMENTS

'When Gregor Samsa woke up one morning from unsettling dreams, he found himself changed in his bed into a monstrous vermin.' ❧ *The Metamorphosis* FRANZ KAFKA

TITLE _____

AUTHOR _____

DATE _____

COMMENTS

TITLE _____

AUTHOR _____

DATE _____

COMMENTS

TITLE _____

AUTHOR _____

DATE _____

COMMENTS

'Ours is essentially a tragic age, so we refuse to take it tragically.'
Lady Chatterley's Lover D H LAWRENCE

BOOKS TO READ

TITLE ——————————————————

AUTHOR ——————————————————

SUBJECT ——————————————————

RECOMMENDED BY ——————————————————

TITLE ——————————————————

AUTHOR ——————————————————

SUBJECT ——————————————————

RECOMMENDED BY ——————————————————

TITLE ——————————————————

AUTHOR ——————————————————

SUBJECT ——————————————————

RECOMMENDED BY ——————————————————

TITLE ————————————————————

AUTHOR ————————————————————

SUBJECT ————————————————————

RECOMMENDED BY ————————————————————

TITLE ————————————————————

AUTHOR ————————————————————

SUBJECT ————————————————————

RECOMMENDED BY ————————————————————

TITLE ————————————————————

AUTHOR ————————————————————

SUBJECT ————————————————————

RECOMMENDED BY ————————————————————

TITLE ——————————————

AUTHOR ——————————————

SUBJECT ——————————————

RECOMMENDED BY ——————————————

TITLE ——————————————

AUTHOR ——————————————

SUBJECT ——————————————

RECOMMENDED BY ——————————————

TITLE ——————————————

AUTHOR ——————————————

SUBJECT ——————————————

RECOMMENDED BY ——————————————

TITLE ———————————————

AUTHOR ———————————————

SUBJECT ———————————————

RECOMMENDED BY ———————————————

TITLE ———————————————

AUTHOR ———————————————

SUBJECT ———————————————

RECOMMENDED BY ———————————————

TITLE ———————————————

AUTHOR ———————————————

SUBJECT ———————————————

RECOMMENDED BY ———————————————

TITLE —————————————————————

AUTHOR —————————————————————

SUBJECT —————————————————————

RECOMMENDED BY —————————————————————

TITLE —————————————————————

AUTHOR —————————————————————

SUBJECT —————————————————————

RECOMMENDED BY —————————————————————

TITLE —————————————————————

AUTHOR —————————————————————

SUBJECT —————————————————————

RECOMMENDED BY —————————————————————

TITLE ——————————————————

AUTHOR ——————————————————

SUBJECT ——————————————————

RECOMMENDED BY ——————————————————

TITLE ——————————————————

AUTHOR ——————————————————

SUBJECT ——————————————————

RECOMMENDED BY ——————————————————

TITLE ——————————————————

AUTHOR ——————————————————

SUBJECT ——————————————————

RECOMMENDED BY ——————————————————

TITLE ―――――――――――――――――――――

AUTHOR ―――――――――――――――――――

SUBJECT ―――――――――――――――――――

RECOMMENDED BY ――――――――――――――――

TITLE ―――――――――――――――――――――

AUTHOR ―――――――――――――――――――

SUBJECT ―――――――――――――――――――

RECOMMENDED BY ――――――――――――――――

TITLE ―――――――――――――――――――――

AUTHOR ―――――――――――――――――――

SUBJECT ―――――――――――――――――――

RECOMMENDED BY ――――――――――――――――

TITLE ——————————

AUTHOR ——————————

SUBJECT ——————————

RECOMMENDED BY ——————————

TITLE ——————————

AUTHOR ——————————

SUBJECT ——————————

RECOMMENDED BY ——————————

TITLE ——————————

AUTHOR ——————————

SUBJECT ——————————

RECOMMENDED BY ——————————

TITLE ————————————————————————

AUTHOR ————————————————————————

SUBJECT ————————————————————————

RECOMMENDED BY ————————————————————————

TITLE ————————————————————————

AUTHOR ————————————————————————

SUBJECT ————————————————————————

RECOMMENDED BY ————————————————————————

TITLE ————————————————————————

AUTHOR ————————————————————————

SUBJECT ————————————————————————

RECOMMENDED BY ————————————————————————

TITLE __Chestnut Tree__

AUTHOR __Charlotte Bingham__

SUBJECT __Family   WW 2__

RECOMMENDED BY __Own purchase.__

TITLE _____

AUTHOR _____

SUBJECT _____

RECOMMENDED BY _____

TITLE _____

AUTHOR _____

SUBJECT _____

RECOMMENDED BY _____

TITLE _____

AUTHOR _____

SUBJECT _____

RECOMMENDED BY _____

TITLE Give Me Tommorrow.

AUTHOR Elzabeth Lord.

SUBJECT Suffragettes.

RECOMMENDED BY _____

TITLE The Palace of Strange Girls

AUTHOR Sally Worboys Day

SUBJECT Blackpool Post WW

RECOMMENDED BY _____

TITLE Paws fo the Proceedings

AUTHOR Deic Longdun

SUBJECT CATS!

RECOMMENDED BY OK as a light read
16/9/09

TITLE A Winters Tale

AUTHOR Trisha Ashley

SUBJECT Heiress to crumbling Pile

RECOMMENDED BY Own Purchase 17/10/09
Nice light read — amusing

TITLE The Laments

AUTHOR George Hagen

SUBJECT

RECOMMENDED BY Own Purchase
Well written but very sad — black humour.

TITLE _Suspicions of Mr Wicher_

AUTHOR _Kate Summerscale_

SUBJECT _Murder - detection_

RECOMMENDED BY _Mum_ _18th July 2008_

Limited enjoyment. Well researched.

TITLE _Tom Bedlam_

AUTHOR _George Hagen_

SUBJECT _London 19th Century_

RECOMMENDED BY _Bargain Books_ _June 09_

Thoroughly enjoyed.
Unusual writing style

TITLE _Sand In My Shoes._

AUTHOR _Joan Rice_

SUBJECT _Diary WW2_

RECOMMENDED BY _Bought Bargain Books_

Diary - irritating. Not 'my thing'

_10.9.09_

TITLE Northanger Abbey

AUTHOR Jane Austen

SUBJECT

RECOMMENDED BY For J.A.Soc Dec. 2008.

TITLE The Return

AUTHOR Victoria Hislop

SUBJECT Spanish Civil War

RECOMMENDED BY Own Choice — not as good as
The Island.

TITLE Silas Marner

AUTHOR George Elliott

SUBJECT

RECOMMENDED BY Book Group June 2009
Enjoyed.

TITLE Observations

AUTHOR Jane Harris

SUBJECT Servant e Mistress —
Relationships . Bessie a Arabella.

RECOMMENDED BY Reading Group Book

TITLE The Riverman

AUTHOR Alex Cray

SUBJECT Thriller

RECOMMENDED BY Reading Group — awful!

TITLE Miss Pettigrew Lives for A Day

AUTHOR Winifred Watson .

SUBJECT 30's — different lives/classes.

RECOMMENDED BY New Books Mag

Fun

Rosamund Lehman
Invitation to Waltz. 30's culture

Dorothy at Book Gp.

O.K

TITLE _Lollipop Shoes_

AUTHOR _Joanne Harris_

SUBJECT _Witches._

RECOMMENDED BY _Didn't enjoy_

✳ TITLE _Atonement_

AUTHOR _____

SUBJECT _Family_

RECOMMENDED BY _Book Group_
                O.K

TITLE _Guernsey Literary & Potato Peel Pie Soc._

AUTHOR _____

SUBJECT _Channel Island WW_

RECOMMENDED BY _Chosen in Waterstones_
                excellent — characterisation.

TITLE _Fruit & Mango (Arrow)_

AUTHOR _David Nobbs_

SUBJECT _____

RECOMMENDED BY _N b M_

TITLE _Mothers Day_

AUTHOR _K. Scott (Hodder)_

SUBJECT _____

RECOMMENDED BY _____

TITLE _____

AUTHOR _____

SUBJECT _____

RECOMMENDED BY _____

www.readersgroupprize.com
www.penguin.co.uk/readers

Reading Exp Database
www.open.ac.uk/Arts/RED/availdle readus.htm